DATE DUE

DEMCO 38-297

ENCYCLOPEDIA of PRESIDENTS

James Carter

Thirty-Ninth President of the United States

By Linda R. Wade

Consultant: Charles Abele, Ph.D.
Social Studies Instructor
Chicago Public School System

CHILDRENS PRESS®

CHICAGO

Jimmy and Rosalynn Carter at the White House

Library of Congress Cataloging-in-Publication Data

Wade, Linda R.
   James Carter / by Linda R. Wade.
      p.   cm. — (Encyclopedia of presidents)
   Includes index.
   Summary: Describes the life and achievements of the relatively
unknown governor from Georgia who became president of the
United States in 1977.
   ISBN 0-516-01372-6
   1.   Carter, Jimmy, 1924-   —Juvenile literature.
2.   Presidents—United States—Biography—Juvenile literature.
3.   United States—Politics and government—1977-1981—
Juvenile literature. [1. Carter, Jimmy, 1924-
2. Presidents.] I. Title. II. Series.
E873.W33   1989
973.926'092—dc20   89-33754
[B]   CIP
[92]   AC

Picture Acknowledgments

AP/Wide World Photos—4, 5, 6, 8, 12, 13 (top),
17, 18 (2 photos), 19 (top), 20, 22, 24, 28, 29,
30, 36, 37, 38, 39, 40, 41 (top), 42 (2 photos),
47, 48, 49, 50, 51, 52 (bottom), 54 (bottom), 55
(top), 56, 57, 58 (bottom), 59 (2 photos), 61, 62,
66 (2 photos), 67 (2 photos), 70 (2 photos), 78
(bottom), 79 (bottom), 82, 84, 85, 86, 88 (2
photos), 89 (2 photos)

Official U.S. Navy Photograph—25, 27

Copyright 1971 The Time Inc. Magazine
Company. Reprinted by Permission.—44

UPI/Bettmann Newsphotos—9 (2 photos), 10, 13
(bottom), 15, 16, 19 (bottom), 34, 41 (bottom),
43, 52 (top), 53, 54 (top), 55 (bottom), 58 (top),
60 (2 photos), 64, 69 (2 photos), 71, 72, 73 (2
photos), 75 (2 photos), 76, 78 (top), 79 (top), 80,
81, 87

U.S. Bureau of Printing and Engraving—2

Cover design and illustration
by Steven Gaston Dobson

Outgoing President Gerald Ford with President-elect Carter on inauguration day

Table of Contents

Chapter 1

"Running for What?"

"Hello, I'm Jimmy Carter, and I'm running for President of the United States. I need your help."

The man who said this again and again, to people all over the country, had a wide smile and kind blue eyes. To most people, he seemed like a nice guy. But most people — and this was a problem — had never heard of Jimmy Carter.

"Who is he?" people wondered. They learned that he was a peanut farmer. They also learned he'd been the governor of Georgia.

"What does he stand for?" people asked themselves. In his speeches, Jimmy Carter told them he wanted everyone who wanted to work to have a job. He believed that oil and gas should be conserved. As governor of Georgia, he had worked for the rights of blacks and other minorities, and he promised to do so again as president.

"He'll never make it," people said. Nobody outside of Georgia had ever heard of him. An editor for the *Atlanta Constitution* used this headline for one of his columns: "Jimmy Carter's Running for What?" The editor went on to say, "Governor Jimmy Carter's timing was just right. The state needed a good belly laugh, and Carter obliged by announcing he would run for president."

Carter takes the oath of office as thirty-ninth president of the United States.

On January 20, 1977, that editor had to eat his words, because on that day, James Earl Carter, Jr. — known to his family and friends and now to the world as "Jimmy" Carter — was sworn in as the thirty-ninth president of the United States.

How did it happen?

Above: Carter delivers his inaugural address, January 20, 1977.
Below: The Carter family leads the inaugural parade.

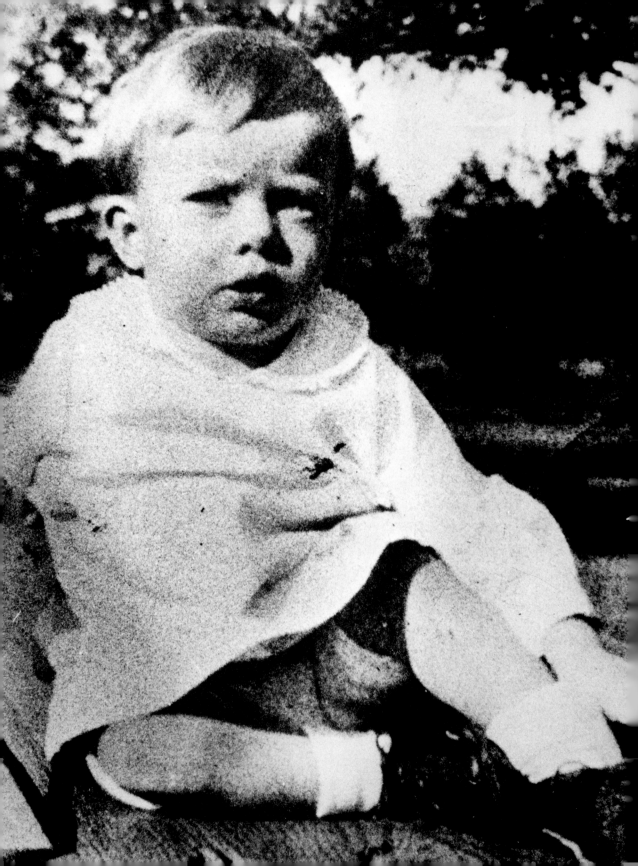

Chapter 2

Growing Up in Plains

James Earl Carter was always called Earl. He met Bessie Lillian Gordy while she was in nurse's training at Wise Hospital in the little town of Plains in southwestern Georgia. Most people called her Lillian. They dated for a year, became engaged, and were married in 1923.

James Earl Carter, Jr., was born nearly a year later on October 1, 1924, in Plains. (To many people, it was simply known as Sumter County.) Later, Earl and Lillian had two girls named Gloria and Ruth and a boy called Billy.

Earl provided quite well for his family. He was a farmer and also ran a farm products store in nearby Archery. The little family lived in a wooden house on a dirt road that led from Savannah to Columbus, Georgia. The house was heated by fireplaces, and Jimmy's mother cooked on a wooden stove. Jimmy's bedroom was in the northeast corner of the house, where there was no heat. His mother made comforters of goose down to keep him warm.

The bathroom was located in the backyard, as was the well. Some time later, running water was installed in the house, along with bathroom fixtures. But water still had to be heated or the family had to take cold showers.

Right: Earl Carter with his children Gloria, Ruth, and Jimmy

Below: Jimmy and Billy Carter with their grandmother in Plains

Opposite page: Jimmy at six months old on his mother Lillian's lap

As in many homes in the 1920s, life centered around the home and family. The workday began at 4:00 A.M. when a large bell clanged, calling all the workers to the barn. By lantern light they loaded their supplies on the wagon, harnessed the mules, and headed out to the red clay fields of cotton, corn, and peanuts. They also planted watermelons, sweet potatoes, and Irish potatoes.

Farm families worked together, and Jimmy's family was no different. Jimmy came to understand what his father needed done and knew what was expected of him. Earl always worked harder than anyone and set a good example for his son. Earl also believed in resting after lunch. Sometimes in the hot summer when there was little breeze, the two of them would stretch out on the bare porch floor and take a short nap. Then it was back to the fields to complete the day's work.

Among other things, the Carters raised chickens on their farm. Jimmy found nests all over the yard when he gathered the eggs. He also had regular chores, which included chopping wood for the fireplaces and stove.

One of Jimmy's jobs was "mopping" cotton. "It was a job for boys and not men, and we despised this task," he wrote later. He made a mixture of arsenic, molasses, and water and, with a rag at the end of a stick, coated each bud of each cotton plant. The object was to kill the boll weevils (insects) that could destroy the cotton. After a while, Jimmy's trousers would be covered with this syrupy mess, and then the flies would swarm around him. At night when he took off his pants, he could stand them in the corner because the legs wouldn't bend.

14

A typical breadline during the Great Depression

Following in his father's footsteps, Jimmy developed a capacity for hard work. At the age of six, he sold twenty bags of peanuts in town each day that he was not helping in the fields. He earned a dollar a day, sometimes five dollars on Saturdays. By the time he was nine, he had saved enough to buy five bales of cotton for five cents a pound. Jimmy stored the bales in his father's warehouse for several years until the price increased to eighteen cents per pound. With the money from this sale he later purchased five houses. He rented them until they were sold in 1949.

The Carters worked hard, but they had a home and plenty to eat. Life was much more difficult for many people in the United States. The economy of the country was at its lowest point in history. This period would become known as the Great Depression. Many people lost their jobs. Businesses and banks failed, causing people to stand in food lines and walk the streets looking for work.

Lillian Carter with her children Gloria and Jimmy

Jimmy Carter started school during this difficult time. He was six years old. The school in Plains was small, and all grades through high school were in the same building.

Miss Julia Coleman was Jimmy's school superintendent and teacher. She became one of the most influential people in his life and encouraged him to learn about music, art, and literature. She also taught him to debate and encouraged him to memorize and recite long poems and chapters from the Bible. He participated in spelling contests and learned to read music.

Jimmy playing in the woods at the age of thirteen

When Jimmy was twelve years old, Miss Coleman asked him to read *War and Peace*, by Leo Tolstoy. Jimmy, thinking that the book was about cowboys and Indians, was excited until he went to the library to check it out. He was surprised to find that it was 1,400 pages long and not about cowboys at all. It was about life in Russia at the time of Napoleon Bonaparte's invasion in 1812. Napoleon was leading the greatest army ever assembled until then, with fighting men from twenty nations. Tolstoy wrote about students, farmers, everyday people, and common soldiers as they struggled for military and political power.

Above: A 1931 snapshot of
Jimmy and his sister Gloria

Left: Eight-year-old Jimmy
with his pet dog Lady

Right: Barefoot Jimmy heads to the fishing hole.

Below: General Napoleon Bonaparte, whose Russian campaign fascinated Carter

Jimmy (top left) holds the flag for a Plains High School program.

Jimmy read the book, not just once, but several times through the years. He began to see how a government should be shaped by the collective wisdom and judgment of the people.

In the eighth grade Jimmy joined the school's debate team. Here the students discussed contemporary social issues, such as whether the United States should send aid to its allies in Europe. Later he also played basketball and baseball, but he was never very good at these sports. He was a fine runner, though, and did very well at track.

At age sixteen, Jimmy was all set to graduate from high school. He was first in his class and would be the valedictorian. Things were going so well that, when some friends asked Jimmy to skip school with them a few days before graduation, he agreed. It was a beautiful afternoon, too nice to spend indoors, so off they went. No one would find out, Jimmy thought. But he and his friends were caught and punished. As a result, Jimmy lost his position as valedictorian. Still, Miss Coleman chose Jimmy to read a speech entitled "The Building of a Community" at the graduation ceremony.

The year was now 1941, and there was a war in Europe. Many people thought that the United States would go to war, too. Jimmy had always hoped to join the navy. His uncle, Tom Gordy, was a sailor and sent postcards from all over the world. Jimmy wanted to have adventures like that, too. He hoped to attend the United States Naval Academy at Annapolis, Maryland. There he would receive a free college education and graduate as a naval officer.

The academy required a course in chemistry that Plains High School did not offer. So after graduation Jimmy enrolled at Georgia Southwestern, a junior college in Americus, Georgia. There he studied chemistry and engineering. During his second semester, he worked as a laboratory assistant so he could learn more. He also played basketball and was a member of the first team.

After his classes at Georgia Southwestern he went on to Georgia Institute of Technology, where he joined the Navy Reserve Officers Training Corps (ROTC). In ROTC he followed a strict schedule of calisthenics and survival training. He also studied general engineering, seamanship, navigation, and other military sciences and was in the top 10 percent of his class. Finally, in 1943, he received a congressional appointment to the United States Naval Academy.

Chapter 3

In the Navy

Jimmy Carter's childhood dream came true when he entered the United States Naval Academy at Annapolis, Maryland, in 1943. Because of his extra training at Georgia Institute of Technology, Jimmy did especially well in electronics, gunnery, and naval tactics. The academy's requirements were quite demanding, and punishments for small infractions were severe.

First-year students were called plebes, and upperclassmen were allowed to embarrass, punish, and torment the plebes as much as they wished. Jimmy needed all his determination to make it through each day.

By his second year at the academy, however, Jimmy was able to find time to become an expert at identifying enemy ships and aircraft. He also took flying lessons. He was beginning to find some of the adventure he had hoped for in the navy.

Two years before graduation, Jimmy's sister Ruth brought her best friend home while he was on leave. Her name was Rosalynn Smith, and Jimmy asked her to go out with him. After the date he told his mother that Rosalynn was the girl he wanted to marry.

Opposite page: Carter in his navy uniform

Fiancée Rosalynn and mother Lillian pin on Carter's bars at his graduation.

They wrote letters while he was away and dated whenever he was home. Jimmy graduated from the academy in June 1946, and a month later, on July 7, Jimmy and Rosalynn were married in the Plains Baptist Church. She was almost nineteen, and he was twenty-two. Sometimes she was able to live with him, but often they were apart because he spent weeks at sea.

When Jimmy was not working or standing guard duty, he often studied. As a result, he became an expert in recognizing ships and planes by memorizing their silhouettes. These images would be flashed on a screen for just a fraction of a second, and Jimmy worked until he had mastered their identity and knew them at a glance.

Carter's battleship, the USS *New York*

During World War II, Jimmy learned to fly seaplanes. His ship, the USS *New York*, was stationed in the North Atlantic when the announcement came that bombs were dropped on Hiroshima and Nagasaki in Japan. This ended the war.

After the war he was assigned to the USS *Wyoming*. This old battleship had been converted into an electronics and gunnery experimental vessel. A year later he was reassigned to the USS *Mississippi*, another seagoing experimental station testing new equipment.

Jimmy applied to and was accepted for submarine training. In the summer of 1948, Jimmy and Rosalynn and their new baby son Jack moved to New London, Connecticut, for six months in officers' training school.

After graduation, Jimmy took his family home to Plains and drove to Los Angeles, shipped his car to Hawaii, and flew out to join the crew of his first submarine assignment aboard the USS *Pomfret*.

The sub left port for the Far East two days later and encountered one of the major storms in Pacific Ocean history. Jimmy was seasick for five days. During that trip he almost lost his life.

The sub had to surface each night to recharge its batteries. One night during the heavy storm, Jimmy was on the bridge holding tightly to an iron pipe when a huge wave rose about six feet over his head. He lost his grip when the wave fell on him, and he was separated from the submarine. He swam and swam before the wave receded and deposited him on top of a gun. He hung on to it and finally lowered himself to the deck. Had the ocean currents been different, he would have been lost at sea.

In 1950, the navy built its first new submarine since the end of World War II. Jimmy was ordered to report to New London as the senior officer for the construction of the USS *K-1*.

The *K-1* was a submarine designed for antisubmarine warfare and would be submerged for long periods of time. He was responsible for the long-range listening sonar, engineering, maintenance, and operating procedures. He learned how to supervise the diving, surfacing, hovering, and other maneuvers. This duty was tough and demanding, but Jimmy loved the challenge.

In 1952, while on the *K-1*, Jimmy applied for an assignment with the atomic submarine division of the Bureau of Ships headed by Admiral Hyman Rickover. Rickover put Jimmy through a grueling interview before accepting him for training as the engineering officer on the nuclear submarine USS *Sea Wolf*.

Admiral Hyman Rickover

During that question-and-answer period, Admiral Rickover asked Jimmy, "How did you stand in your class at the Naval Academy?" Jimmy proudly replied, "Sir, I stood fifty-ninth in a class of 820." The admiral looked at him for a long time, then asked, "Did you do your best?" Suddenly Jimmy thought of the times when he could have worked harder and studied even more. He finally confessed, "No, sir, I didn't always do my best." Admiral Rickover turned his chair around to end the interview and asked one final question. "Why not?"

Carter (standing) aboard a submarine in 1952

Even though Admiral Rickover accepted Jimmy for his program, these questions haunted Carter. He read and studied more in the fields of mathematics, nuclear physics, and atomic technology. Jimmy later wrote that Rickover "had a profound effect on my life—perhaps more than anyone except my own parents. . . . He expected the maximum from us, but he always contributed more." He made his men want to do their best.

During these years in the navy, two more little boys were born in the Carter home. James Earl III, better known as Chip, was born in 1950. The last son was born in 1952. His name was Donnell Jeffrey, and they called him Jeff. Their oldest boy, John William, they had nicknamed Jack soon after he was born.

Jimmy's father became ill with cancer near the end of 1952. Jimmy requested and received an extended leave to

James Earl Carter, Sr.

go home to Plains. Earl and Jimmy enjoyed many hours of talking and being together. Earl had been elected to the Georgia House of Representatives, so they talked about politics as well as farming. On July 23, 1953, Earl Carter died at the age of fifty-nine.

Jimmy and Rosalynn discussed the future and disagreed upon what they should do. Jimmy felt a responsibility to his family and neighbors, for he knew his father had been a mainstay in the community. He saw that there were no other family members who could run the business. Rosalynn felt he should continue with his naval career. After pondering the situation for many difficult days, he resigned from the navy with the rank of lieutenant senior grade. With Rosalynn and his three little boys, he moved back to Plains and prepared for the next step in his career.

Left to right: Ruth Carter Stapleton (sister); Governor Jimmy Carter; Lillian Carter (mother); Billy Carter (brother); Mrs. Walter Spann (family friend)

Chapter 4

The Businessman
and Civic Leader

Jimmy Carter began his adjustment back to community living by talking to experienced farmers. He found that many changes had occurred during the eleven years since he had worked on the family farm. Since World War II, Sumter County had been producing more peanuts than cotton. Because of this, farming techniques had changed. The land around Plains is primarily red clay. Farmers had to know much more about agriculture to obtain a good peanut harvest.

To learn about current farming procedures, Jimmy took some short courses at the Agricultural Experiment Station in Tifton, Georgia. He read books and talked to the county agent. After examining his farming choices, Jimmy decided to grow certified seed peanuts on his farm. He also took charge of his father's peanut warehouse, which had become important in the community.

Rosalynn, too, was settling into the business. She handled the books, learning accounting as she went along. Sometimes she and Jimmy worked eighteen hours a day.

A drought in 1954 made life difficult for the farmers and businesspeople of Plains. Several of the area farmers who had purchased their seed and fertilizer from Earl Carter expected to repay him when their crops were sold. Now they were unable to do so, and Jimmy netted less than two hundred dollars for the year. The debts were extended to the following year. Many of these farmers were poor and black, and Jimmy wanted to help them.

Some of the farmers in the area were sharecroppers. These are farmers who grow crops on another person's land. They usually share the crops with the owner. The sharecropper supplies all the labor, and the landowner supplies the land, a house, and farming equipment. By extending their debts, Carter enabled the sharecroppers to keep their homes.

Slowly their business prospered, and the Carters became more active in the community. They put six-year-old Jack in the school where Miss Julia Coleman was still teaching, and they joined the Plains Parent-Teacher Association. Jimmy was elected vice-president of the Plains Lions Club and helped in the drive to raise money for a community swimming pool.

On May 17, 1954, during Jimmy's first year back in Plains, the United States Supreme Court made an important decision in a case called *Brown versus Board of Education*. The court ruled that so-called "separate but equal" schools for whites and blacks was unconstitutional because it did not actually provide equal education opportunities for all students.

Most people in Georgia opposed the court's ruling and

declared that it did not apply in their state. Those people in Plains who were against any change organized the White Citizens' Council to keep black children out of the white schools.

Jimmy Carter refused to join the council. Several prominent people from the city tried to persuade him, but he held firm. He told them he would rather leave Plains than join such an unfair organization. As a result, a boycott was organized against his business. It lasted for a few weeks, but gradually most people came back to the Carter warehouse.

Jimmy had attended church and Sunday school most of his life. Now that he was back in his hometown, he taught a boys' Sunday school class at the Plains Baptist Church every week and was active in the Men's Brotherhood organization.

Jimmy was also a deacon in the church. Once he missed a meeting at which an important vote was taken. The church officers had voted that black people could not attend the regular church services. They could only come into the church for funerals. Jimmy did not believe this was fair. He went to the church conference and made a speech against the decision.

As a member of the local school board, Jimmy heard the other members argue that "separate but equal" schools were good for both blacks and whites. But he also saw that equality was usually lost in the shuffle. He said and did little to change things for black people in Plains at that time, but he was beginning to look at himself and others in a different way.

Chapter 5

The Politician

Jimmy Carter had listened as his father and other businessmen discussed different political candidates. In 1952, Earl Carter had been elected to the Georgia state legislature. Although Earl served less than a year before his death, Jimmy was proud of his father's accomplishments. Upon Earl's death, Jimmy became so busy with his new responsibilities that he had little time to think of political ambitions.

Early in 1962, however, some friends asked Jimmy if he would run for the state senate. He declined at first but later reconsidered. He had the family business in good shape. Rosalynn had been working with him and knew the business so that she could take over in his absence. He felt he needed a change, and he also thought he might be able to accomplish some of his father's goals in the state senate. On September 30, he announced his candidacy.

Jimmy Carter campaigned hard. On election day he was still shaking hands and kissing babies. When the votes were counted, it appeared that he had lost. Then it was discovered that a campaign worker named Joe Hurst had committed some illegal practices in Quitman County.

Carter (center right) being sworn in to the Georgia state senate in 1963

Joe had met the voters at the polling-place door, put his arm around their shoulders, and told them to vote for Homer Moore, Jimmy's opponent. During an investigation, it was found that Joe Hurst had even voted on behalf of dead people and those who were in prison. Jimmy Carter was finally declared the winner.

As a state senator, he worked hard to reduce waste in government and to take away some of the unnecessary special privileges some politicians enjoyed.

In 1966, State Senator Jimmy Carter became a candidate for governor of Georgia, but he lost. Georgia changes

Carter casts his vote for governor of Georgia.

governors every four years, so the next morning he told reporters that he was the first announced candidate for governor in 1970. During those four years, the people of Georgia found out that Jimmy Carter was serious about what he had said. He met with many groups of people and talked with them about their concerns.

He also had something else to talk about. Jimmy and Rosalynn became parents again. Amy Lynn was born on October 19, 1967. The family was proud and happy, and this spurred his campaign on. When the vote of 1970 was counted, Jimmy Carter had a landslide victory.

Carter takes the oath of office as governor of Georgia.

Now Governor Carter could make a difference in the lives of those who were in need of help. He told his fellow Georgians that "the time for racial discrimination is over. . . . No poor, rural, weak or black person should ever have to bear the additional burden of being deprived of the opportunity of an education, a job, or simple justice."

As governor, Carter's top priority was the reorganization of the Georgia state government. Under this program, three hundred state agencies, boards, commissions and departments were consolidated into twenty-two major agencies. One of the most important changes was a law to provide equal state aid to schools in the wealthy and poor areas of Georgia. He also set up community centers for retarded children and increased education programs for

Dr. Martin Luther King, Jr., president of the Southern Christian Leadership Conference

people in prison. His plans included environmental protection laws, more reasonable utility rates, and conservation of energy.

While he was governor, Carter opened many job opportunities for blacks in the Georgia state government. During his administration, the number of black state employees rose by about 40 percent. He had the portraits of important black people hung in the Georgia state capitol. They included Dr. Martin Luther King, Jr., a famous civil rights leader, and Bishop Henry Turner and Lucy Laney, two black people from Georgia who had been important to its history. Until these portraits were hung, there had been pictures of only white people hanging at the capitol.

Carter, in East Berlin, Germany, observes the Berlin Wall.

Carter also visited Europe and the Middle East to promote Georgia business. He promoted movie making in Georgia and assisted established businesses in the state. One day a month, he made himself available to anyone who wanted to visit him in his office.

He was a good governor. Several national newspapers and magazines featured articles about Jimmy Carter. But almost no one expected him to run for president of the United States.

Above: Carter and Secretary of State Henry Kissinger discuss the opening session of the Organization of American States, in Atlanta.

Right: Governor Carter giving a press conference in 1972

Above: Carter up to his knees
in peanuts in a Plains warehouse

Left: Carter preparing a statement
for the press during his campaign
for governor of Georgia

Opposite page: Carter at the
national governors' conference
in Houston, Texas, in 1972

NATIONAL
GOVERNORS' CONFERENCE
TEXAS 1972

GOVERNOR
JIMMY CARTER
GEORGIA

GOVERNOR

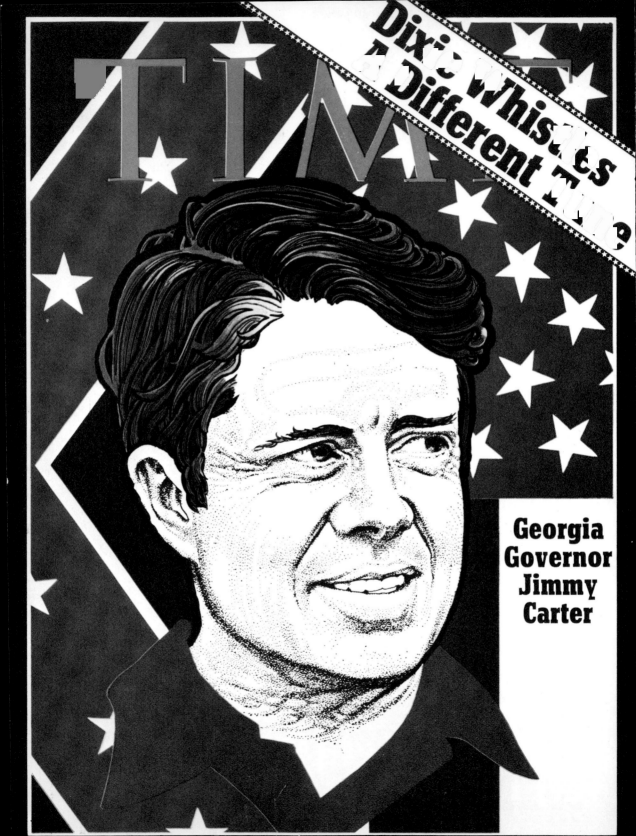

TIME

Dixie Whistles A Different Tune

Georgia
Governor
Jimmy
Carter

Chapter 6

The Candidate

Because of his call for racial justice, the *Washington Post* and *Life* magazine called Jimmy Carter a representative of the "New South." He was pictured on the cover of a May 1971 issue of *Time* magazine with the caption, "Dixie Whistles a Different Tune." Carter did not always appreciate being singled out as the one to speak for desegregation, but this issue had at least introduced his name outside of Georgia and given him national attention.

Since becoming governor, Carter had headed the 1972 Democratic Governors' Campaign Committee, which helped elect the party's candidates for governor throughout the United States. He also served as chairman of the Democratic National Campaign Committee in 1974. These activities helped to broaden his acquaintance with political forces outside of Georgia.

Even so, little notice was taken when Jimmy Carter gathered together his entire family in 1974 and announced that he was going to be a presidential candidate. Nevertheless, Jimmy went to work training for this new job. He took speech lessons so that his speaking voice would not sound so southern. He read the nation's major newspapers and he listened to newsmen. Gradually Carter developed his own ideas about what the country needed.

Opposite page: Carter on the cover
of *Time* magazine, May 31, 1971

Georgia friends were called together for support. At first they were doubtful, but as Jimmy talked they began to get enthused. The Watergate scandal, which had caused President Richard Nixon to resign in 1974, was still on the minds of Americans.

As an outsider to Watergate, Jimmy could claim no involvement. He would bring fresh ideas and new people to Washington. Certainly the country had problems, but Carter believed he was the one to solve them. When he finished talking to his group, they gave him a standing ovation. They would work hard for him.

Carter had a plan. He assigned a campaign worker to each state. This person was to contact that state's Democratic party chairman and get Jimmy Carter invited to speak to the state caucus, answer questions, and get acquainted. Here, Carter's work with the Governor's Campaign Committee began paying off. There were people in about thirty states who had used Carter's help. Jimmy's Georgia friends were convinced that he could become president if he became better known.

Perhaps so, but there were disappointing times ahead. At a press conference in Philadelphia, only the candidate and his press secretary, Jody Powell, showed up. Jimmy Carter was not very big news.

Rosalynn and the three boys traveled, too, each going in different directions. Then they returned home to Plains, where they discussed the places they had visited and the people's reactions. Jimmy once said, "While the others have been building a money base, we've been building a people base."

Hamilton Jordan, campaign
worker and later White
House chief of staff

Preparation for the 1976 primary elections began early.
Hamilton Jordan, who was a close and trusted friend of
Jimmy's, gathered a group of Carter volunteers from
neighboring cities. On January 4 at 7:00 A.M., about one
hundred of these Georgians, equipped with hats, gloves,
boots, and overcoats, met at the Atlanta airport. Their plan
was to invade Manchester, New Hampshire, to meet and
talk with voters about Jimmy Carter. These volunteers
were so dedicated that they paid their own expenses.

The airport runway in Manchester was coated with solid
ice when the plane skidded to a stop. The Georgians
stepped out into a temperature colder than what most of
them had ever experienced. Now they knew why Jordan
had told them to bring so many cold-weather clothes. It
was 20 degrees, with a windchill factor of 10 below zero.

Carter and supporters celebrate a victory in the primary elections.

After detailed instruction, the volunteers were ready to start. In Manchester, Nashua, and surrounding towns, they went to every home that had at least one registered Democrat in it. They introduced themselves and told how they had come all the way from Georgia to tell the New Hampshire people about their friend Jimmy Carter. Their goal was to contact a total of 25,000 households. Each person was to reach 55 households per day. When possible, they met workers during shift changes at business establishments. In the evenings, they sent follow-up letters along with additional Carter information to those with whom they had spoken that day.

These volunteers became known as the Peanut Brigade. Largely because of their efforts, Jimmy Carter won the

Carter campaigning in New York's Harlem district

New Hampshire primary. The media people now took greater notice. Newspapers carried pictures, and television news covered more Carter activities.

Soon he had won the primaries in Florida, Iowa, Maine, Oklahoma, and Vermont. Then came Wisconsin. The Peanut Brigade was sent to Green Bay. On election night Morris Udall claimed victory early in the evening, but when the Green Bay area votes were counted, Carter had won. The *Milwaukee Sentinel* changed its headlines from "Carter Upset by Udall" to "Carter Edges Out Udall." The Peanut Brigade had done it again. Without this dedicated Georgia bunch, Carter probably would have remained unknown to most of America.

Carter campaigning in Youngstown, Ohio, before the Ohio primary

Other state primaries were now well under way, with more states leaning toward Carter. Even though he lost both California and New Jersey, the win in Ohio gave him 1,260 of the 1,505 delegates he needed to win the Democratic presidential nomination. One by one, additional states threw their support to Jimmy. Other candidates dropped out of the running and released their delegates to the former Georgia governor.

By June 9, 1976, a month before the Democratic national convention in New York City, the 1,505 delegates were assured. Carter then went to work interviewing potential vice-presidents. He finally chose Walter Mondale, a senator from Minnesota.

A grinning peanut, representing Carter, at the Democratic convention

On the final night of the Democratic convention in August, the new Carter-Mondale team took the floor. Walter Mondale was introduced first, and he spoke to the delegates. Then Jimmy Carter appeared before the convention for the first time. His smile was warm, and so were his words. "Hello, I'm Jimmy Carter," he said, "and I'm running for President of the United States."

Jimmy spoke of a hurting nation, torn apart by Watergate, and told the cheering Democrats that it was a time for healing. He promised to be more responsive to the people, reduce the size and number of federal agencies, open the administration, and better the economy by creating jobs. Immediately after the convention, Carter began his final campaign effort.

Above: Carter accepts his nomination, July 15, 1976.
Below: Carter and running mate, Senator Walter Mondale

Republican candidates Gerald Ford (right) and Robert Dole (left)

The Republicans nominated Gerald Ford, who had become president when Richard Nixon resigned. Senator Robert Dole from Kansas was chosen as his running mate. When he accepted the Republican nomination, Ford said that he was "eager to go before the American people and debate the real issues face-to-face with Jimmy Carter."

In some opinion polls, Carter was leading by as much as 30 percentage points. Ford felt that he could catch up by debating Carter. It was decided that there would be three presidential debates and one vice-presidential debate.

The first debate took place in Philadelphia on September 23 and focused on domestic issues and economic policy. Carter appeared nervous at first but settled down to a comfortable routine. The Roper poll announced the next day that 39 percent of the American people thought Ford did the best and 31 percent gave the edge to Carter.

Above: Presidential candidate Carter holds a baby outside the Plains Baptist Church.

Left: In a field in Plains at sunrise, candidate Carter appears on NBC's _Today_ show.

Top: Carter and Mondale give an informal press conference in Plains.

Bottom: Carter tries on a sombrero at a Mexican Independence Day celebration.

McLean County Unit #5
Carlock IMC - 105

Presidential candidates Carter and Ford at a debate in Philadelphia

Between the first and second debate, the polls showed that Carter was slipping. This made the Republicans feel more comfortable with the second debate. They believed that Ford's career in the House and his experience as president would help him to outperform Carter. What happened was a surprise to all.

The second debate was held in San Francisco on October 6. All questions from the panel dealt with foreign policy. President Ford did not do as well as expected. He made a big mistake when he said that many of the Eastern European nations were not dominated by the Soviet Union. Ford's error, together with a change in Carter's style, gave the debate to Carter. This time he was more aggressive with his answers and put President Ford on the defensive.

The first vice-presidential debate was scheduled for October 15 in Houston, Texas. Most people felt that Walter

Vice-presidential candidates Mondale (left) and Dole (right) debating

Mondale did better than Republican Robert Dole did, and the Carter-Mondale ticket gained a few points in the polls.

The last presidential debate took place on October 22 in Williamsburg, Virginia. Questions could cover any subject. The press called this debate "the rubber match" because neither candidate scored a significant victory.

By October 29, the Harris poll scored Carter 45 and Ford 44, with Ford still picking up votes. This was going to be an election too close for anyone to call. Even the television news teams refused to speculate on the outcome.

Americans voted on Tuesday, November 2. It was not until the predawn hours of the next day that they knew their next president would be Jimmy Carter. It was the closest election since 1960, when John F. Kennedy defeated Richard M. Nixon. This time Americans had brought a peanut farmer from Georgia to the White House.

The Carters and the Mondales acknowledge cheers at the Democratic
national convention in New York City on July 16, 1976.

Above: The Carter family eating box lunches on a campaign tour in Texas
Below: Carter, in Plains, holds up a local newspaper proclaiming his victory.

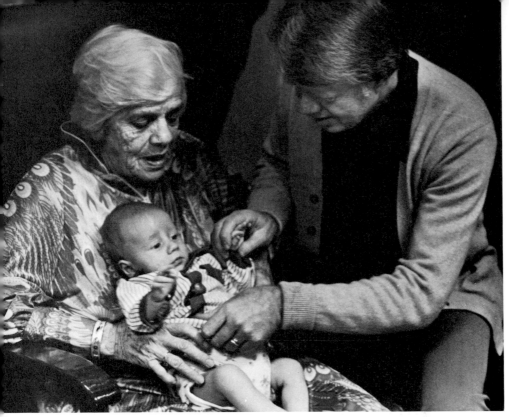

Above: Miss Lillian, Carter, and brother Billy's baby, Earl. Below: Jimmy and Billy
Right: Daughter Amy and grandson Jason in a treehouse on the White House lawn

Chapter 7

The President

Bitter cold Washington weather chilled thousands of people who came to watch the inauguration of Jimmy Carter as thirty-ninth president of the United States. The crowds cheered as they heard him say he wanted to be a "president of the people." Later, President and Mrs. Carter, together with their family, entered the presidential limousine and began to move toward the White House. Soon the vehicle stopped, and Americans were happy to see the president and his family exit the car. With a big smile, the new president took his wife's hand and began walking from the Capitol to the White House, where they would live for the next four years.

President Carter soon went to work on the problems that faced the nation. In his first day on the job he gave a presidential pardon to draft evaders of the Vietnam era. Unemployment was high, so to create more jobs Carter pushed for welfare and tax reform. He also pushed for a less-polluted environment. The new president was interested in many things: the American farmer, the protection of whales, the nuclear submarine corps, and the conservation of water.

Bert Lance testifies in the Senate before his appointment as budget director.

As President Carter saw it, the most serious problem in the United States was the energy crisis. He encouraged Americans to turn their thermostats down and to drive more energy-efficient cars. James Schlesinger, former CIA chief and secretary of defense, was chosen to head up the newly developed Department of Energy.

By mid-1977, President Carter had begun to lose some of his popularity with the American people. He had chosen a friend from Georgia, Bert Lance, to head up the Office of Management and Budget. During the summer, newspaper and TV reports announced that Lance was suspected of illegal banking practices while president of a Georgia bank. Even though he was innocent, Lance resigned in the face of the media attacks. This was a serious matter. Jimmy Carter had talked of bringing honesty and morality to Washington, and now it seemed that his choices were no better than those of other presidents.

Other plans went astray, too. President Carter's crusade for human rights, at home and in other countries, angered the Soviet Union. Carter's goal to eliminate nuclear weapons was also opposed by many people in both the United States and abroad. An example was the strategic arms limitation treaty (SALT II) between Soviet president Leonid Brezhnev and President Carter to limit the creation of new nuclear weapons. The treaty was never approved by the U.S. Senate because some senators supposed it gave an unfair advantage to the Russians.

Conflicts also began to arise over the Panama Canal. The Panamanian people did not want the canal controlled by the United States and threatened to sabotage the waterway. President Carter pushed through Congress a treaty that would give ownership of the canal to Panama on December 31, 1999. The president thought that the goodwill of the Latin American country was worth more than technical control of the canal.

In 1973, a group of countries in the Middle East had formed the Organization of Petroleum Exporting Countries (OPEC). This organization raised the price of oil. As a result, the American economy slumped. Oil prices continued to climb, and the inflation rate rose to double-digit levels. Interest rates rose so high that few people could afford to borrow money to build new homes. Businesses could not borrow to expand or to buy new equipment. Congress eventually approved some of President Carter's measures for fuel conservation and the development of new sources of energy. Their effects, however, were slow to be seen.

Above: Carter meets with Soviet president Leonid Brezhnev in 1979.
Below: Carter and Panama president Omar Torrijos after signing the Panama Canal treaty

**Above: Carter with foreign policy adviser Zbigniew Brzezinski (left) and
Secretary of State Cyrus Vance (right).   Below: Typical scene during a gas shortage**

In foreign affairs, President Carter did have some success in the Middle East. Throughout 1977 he insisted that he would settle for nothing less than a comprehensive peace in the troubled Middle East. But peace talks had been unsuccessful, and peace efforts were receiving many unfavorable reactions.

Finally the president decided to take a big chance. On August 5, 1978, he invited Egyptian president Anwar Sadat and Israeli prime minister Menachem Begin to the United States. The three would meet at the presidential retreat, Camp David, to work on the Middle Eastern situation. (Camp David is a 143-acre presidential hideaway located in the Catoctin Mountains in Maryland.) Begin and Sadat immediately accepted.

The meetings started on September 5. For thirteen days, no information was given to the press. The three leaders alternately debated and accepted and refused ideas for peace in the Middle East.

During the discussions, Carter talked first to one leader and then to the other. Sometimes the three of them talked together. After eight days, Carter determined that the issues required separate negotiations; a comprehensive peace settlement was impossible.

Finally, with a deadline set for the talks to end, workable compromises were made. The summit ended on September 17, 1978. There were still hard negotiations ahead, but a long-term framework had been put in place. Finally, on March 26, 1979, Begin and Sadat signed a treaty called the Camp David Accord. It guaranteed peace between Israel and Egypt.

Carter at Camp David with Anwar Sadat (left) and Menachem Begin (right)

The Camp David Accord gave the Carter presidency a much needed boost. According to the Gallup poll, his popularity had dwindled such that only 38 percent of Americans approved of his administration. Now it climbed to 51 percent. Senator William Roth of Delaware sponsored a resolution that President Carter be recommended for the Nobel Peace Prize for his peacemaking efforts.

Meanwhile, another crisis was brewing, and this one would be more difficult to solve.

Above: Egypt's Sadat, Carter, and Israel's Begin meet at Camp David.
Below: Sadat, Carter, and Begin shake hands after announcing their accords.

Begin, Carter, and Sadat stand for the national anthem at a Marine dress parade.

The Ayatollah Khomeini in 1979

The government of Iran, under the leadership of its shah, had been friendly with the United States for thirty-seven years. In fact, Iran was one of America's important sources of foreign oil. When the Iranian government was taken over by the Ayatollah Khomeini in February 1979, the shah fled the country. Many United States government officials encouraged President Carter to invite the shah to the United States. Carter opposed this because he wanted to keep alive the chance for establishing relations with the new government. President Sadat took some of the pressure off Carter by inviting the shah to visit Egypt. King Hassan of Morocco also let the shah visit for a time. Then he went to the Bahamas and finally to Mexico. No country wanted him for long because of the unrest in Iran.

Above: Iranians greet the Ayatollah on his return from 15 years of exile.
Below: Anwar Sadat welcomes the shah of Iran on his arrival for a two-day visit.

After the shah had been in Mexico for a few months, word came to Washington that he was critically ill with cancer and needed medical treatment available only in the United States. The president was still against letting the shah come to the United States but, on humanitarian principles, permitted him to enter the country. This news enraged the religious militants of the new Iranian government. In protest against Carter's decision, they stormed the U.S. embassy in Teheran, Iran, on November 4, 1979, and took ninety hostages, sixty-three of them American employees.

Thus the darkest year in the Carter administration began.

After a while it became apparent that there was no quick solution. Other hostages had been captured before and then released a short time later. Now, at any moment the Carter people expected news from Teheran saying that all the hostages were on their way home.

But one week stretched into two weeks and then a month. The president was expected to do something that would restore national honor and bring the captives home. But what? Carter took the only route he could. He started the difficult business of negotiation through a mediator, the North African country of Algeria.

Occasionally a picture of a handcuffed, blindfolded hostage was released to the press. A few of the hostages were released when they became ill. However, most of the news from Iran was of militants shouting "Death to Carter" and "Death to the shah" as they burned the United States flag.

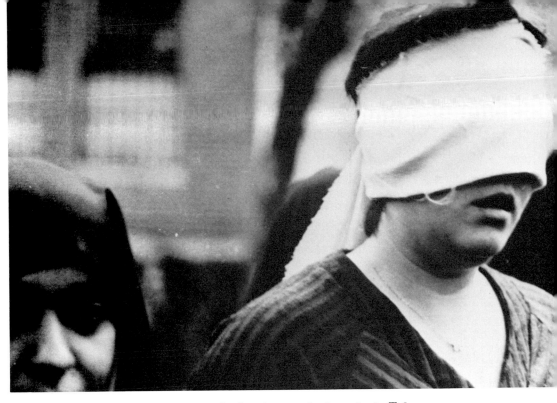

Above: A woman held hostage by Iranian revolutionaries in Teheran
Below: American hostages being paraded by their militant Iranian captors

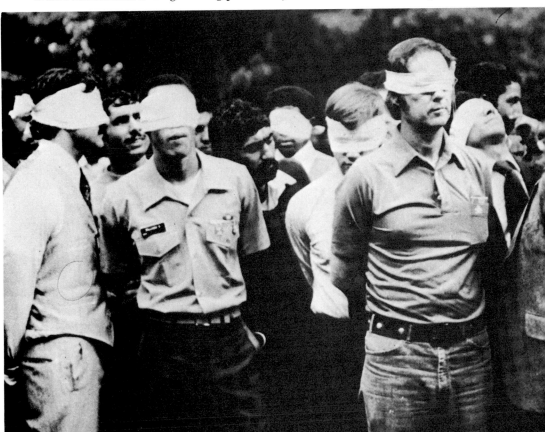

Wreckage of the attempted rescue mission to Iran

In a desperate attempt, President Carter authorized a military force to try a secret rescue. A sudden dust storm caused several helicopters to crash and turned the military operation into a fiasco. Eight marines died and Iranians publicly disgraced their bodies. Negotiations stalled but were then resumed.

Although the hostage negotiations took much of President Carter's time, other events were making news.

In January 1979, Deputy Prime Minister Teng of China began a nine-day state visit to the United States. During his three days with President Carter, scientific and cultural exchanges were agreed upon.

On March 28, 1979, America's worst nuclear accident occurred at Three Mile Island near Harrisburg, Pennsylvania. Mechanical and human failures resulted in a breakdown of the reactor's core cooling system. Scientists and technicians succeeded in preventing a core meltdown, which might have released radiation into the air. The plant remained closed for many years.

The miseries of 1979 spilled into 1980, when the Soviet Union invaded Afghanistan early in January. President Carter retaliated by delaying the opening of a new Soviet consulate in New York City and a U.S. consulate in Kiev. He canceled cultural exchanges and barred new sales of high technology and other strategic goods. He curtailed fishing rights of Russian trawlers in American waters and cut grain sales to Russia by 17 million metric tons. If these actions did not stop the invasion, the president said, the United States would boycott the 1980 Summer Olympics, which were to be held in Moscow. Experts said that an effective boycott would be a political blow to the Soviets, who had wanted to be an Olympic host. A *Newsweek* poll taken soon after the invasion showed that the nation was strongly behind the president.

Carter's cutback of grain sales to Russia resulted in hurting American farmers. Overnight the price of grain dropped from $4.00 a bushel to $3.60. Many grain elevators and farmers' cooperatives suspended purchases, and those who continued to buy reduced the prices they offered. No one approved of the Soviet Union's invasion of Afghanistan, but Americans wondered how much more they would be affected.

Left: Carter and Chinese
Vice Premier Teng Hsiao-
Ping shaking hands outside
the White House

Below: Carter and Teng
sign scientific, cultural,
and consular agreements
in the East Wing of the
White House.

**Above: An aerial view of the Three Mile Island nuclear power plant
Below: Soviet tanks take positions outside Kabul, Afghanistan, January 7, 1980.**

Reagan delivers his acceptance speech for his presidential nomination.

A presidential election was coming up in 1980, and the Democrats rallied behind Jimmy Carter as their candidate once more. The Republicans chose California governor Ronald Reagan, who promised an economic turnaround and jobs for all. His battle cry was "less federal control."

President Carter spoke to Americans about his goals for the country and his accomplishments; he debated Ronald Reagan and continually sought to bring the hostages home. But nothing happened. The year wore on, and neither the cutbacks nor the Olympic boycott could budge the Russians out of Afghanistan. Americans lost confidence in President Carter. As a result, Ronald Reagan won a landslide victory in November 1980.

Before his term ended, President Carter pressed to complete several of his goals. He persuaded Congress to pass

American hostages released from Iran arrive in West Germany on their way home.

the remaining points of his energy program and two important environmental protection laws. One dealt with cleaning up toxic wastes, and the other law permanently protected 150 million acres of wilderness land in Alaska.

Even with these accomplishments, Carter's primary desire was to obtain release for the hostages. At 2:00 A.M. on January 19, 1981, Iran signed a release agreement. But it was not until 8:00 A.M. on inauguration day that the hostages boarded a plane for home. Still, they were not permitted to leave the Iranian runway. Then, just moments after Ronald Reagan was sworn in as president, the remaining fifty-two hostages were released after 444 days of captivity.

It was a bittersweet victory for the now former president Carter.

Jimmy and Rosalynn Carter wave from the podium at the 1984 Democratic convention.

Chapter 8

Back Home Again

After the inauguration of Ronald Reagan, Jimmy Carter, together with his family and closest aides, left Washington in the presidential jet, Air Force One. They went home—but for only one day.

On January 21, Mr. Carter was on his way to Germany as President Reagan's emissary. It seemed only right that he should welcome the hostages back to freedom.

Upon returning to Plains, the Carters prepared for a vacation in the Virgin Islands. For the first time in many years, they were free from the pressures of politics.

Jimmy Carter did not stop caring about his fellow Americans once he was out of office. He went on to find many other ways to help people.

The Carter Center, which he founded at Emory University in Atlanta, includes Carter's presidential library and museum. In this beautiful building are pictures of Jimmy Carter and the people who shaped his life. A replica of the Oval Office lets the visitor enter into the complex world of an American president. Elegant objects from foreign leaders, as well as handmade gifts from the American people, are displayed. Lectures and discussions on foreign and domestic issues are also held at the center.

Carter doing volunteer carpentry in a tenement building in New York City

Through Global 2000 Inc. and the Carter-Menil Human Rights Foundation, Carter continued to talk about environmental and human rights issues throughout the world.

Jimmy Carter also became a regular volunteer for Habitat for Humanity. This is a nonprofit organization that helps build homes for the needy in the United States and in undeveloped countries. It is based in Americus, Georgia, only nine miles from Plains, and has offices in more than three hundred U.S. cities and twenty-five offices in cities in developing countries. Habitat has placed over two thousand low-income families in quality homes in the United States.

Installing a sliding door in a Habitat for Humanity building project

Volunteers—with former President Carter as one of them—do the construction work and pay for or donate many of the building materials, thus keeping housing costs down. Habitat then makes interest-free loans to families so they can buy the moderately priced homes. When the loans are repaid, the money is used to construct more homes for the poor. As Habitat for Humanity volunteers, both Jimmy and Rosalynn Carter worked in several cities over the years.

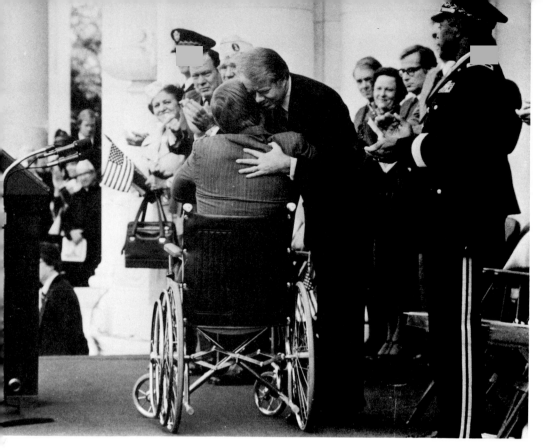

Carter embraces Max Cleland at Veterans Day ceremonies.

Since leaving the presidency, Carter wrote several books, including *Keeping Faith: Memoirs of a President* (1982) and *The Blood of Abraham* (1985). He also published articles about his hobbies, fly fishing and woodworking. Both Mr. and Mrs. Carter resumed teaching Sunday school at the Baptist church in Plains, and Jimmy took up his position again as a deacon in the church.

Jimmy Carter served the United States as president during a difficult time. His final visitor in the Oval Office was Max Cleland, a Vietnam veteran, a triple amputee, and head of the Veterans Administration. He gave the outgoing president a plaque inscribed with words of Thomas Jefferson: "I have the consolation to reflect that during my

Jimmy and Rosalynn preview the Carter Presidential Center in Atlanta.

administration not a drop of the blood of a single citizen was shed by the sword of war." Through all the hardships of the Carter administration, peace was maintained and even enhanced through the Camp David Accord.

Jimmy Carter was a simple peanut farmer from the Deep South who believed he could lead the American people. On the night President Carter was defeated for his second term in office he said, "I've not achieved all I set out to do; perhaps no one ever does. But we have faced the tough issues. We've stood for and we've fought for and we have achieved some very important goals for our country." History will confirm the significance of President Jimmy Carter's deeds.

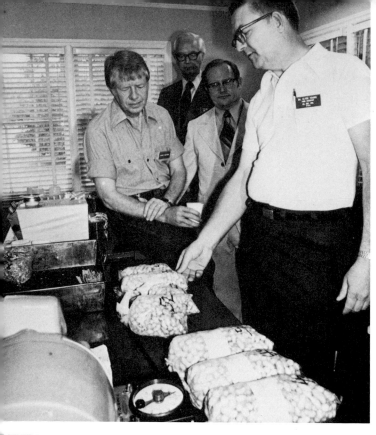

Left: Carter examines peanuts at Georgia Southwestern Agricultural Experiment Station in Plains.

Below: Carter arrives in Frankfurt, Germany, to welcome freed hostages.

Above: A troubled President Carter answers press questions about hostages in Iran.
Below: The official portrait of President and Mrs. Carter, issued by the White House

Chronology of American History

(Shaded area covers events in James Carter's lifetime.)

About A.D. 982 — Eric the Red, born in Norway, reaches Greenland in one of the first European voyages to North America.

About 1000 — Leif Ericson (Eric the Red's son) leads what is thought to be the first European expedition to mainland North America; Leif probably lands in Canada.

1492 — Christopher Columbus, seeking a sea route from Spain to the Far East, discovers the New World.

1497 — John Cabot reaches Canada in the first English voyage to North America.

1513 — Ponce de Léon explores Florida in search of the fabled Fountain of Youth.

1519-1521 — Hernando Cortés of Spain conquers Mexico.

1534 — French explorers led by Jacques Cartier enter the Gulf of St. Lawrence in Canada.

1540 — Spanish explorer Francisco Coronado begins exploring the American Southwest, seeking the riches of the mythical Seven Cities of Cibola.

1565 — St. Augustine, Florida, the first permanent European town in what is now the United States, is founded by the Spanish.

1607 — Jamestown, Virginia, is founded, the first permanent English town in the present-day U.S.

1608 — Frenchman Samuel de Champlain founds the village of Quebec, Canada.

1609 — Henry Hudson explores the eastern coast of present-day U.S. for the Netherlands; the Dutch then claim parts of New York, New Jersey, Delaware, and Connecticut and name the area New Netherland.

1619 — The English colonies' first shipment of black slaves arrives in Jamestown.

1620 — English Pilgrims found Massachusetts' first permanent town at Plymouth.

1621 — Massachusetts Pilgrims and Indians hold the famous first Thanksgiving feast in colonial America.

1623 — Colonization of New Hampshire is begun by the English.

1624 — Colonization of present-day New York State is begun by the Dutch at Fort Orange (Albany).

1625 — The Dutch start building New Amsterdam (now New York City).

1630 — The town of Boston, Massachusetts, is founded by the English Puritans.

1633 — Colonization of Connecticut is begun by the English.

1634 — Colonization of Maryland is begun by the English.

1636 — Harvard, the colonies' first college, is founded in Massachusetts. Rhode Island colonization begins when Englishman Roger Williams founds Providence.

1638 — Delaware colonization begins as Swedes build Fort Christina at present-day Wilmington.

1640 — Stephen Daye of Cambridge, Massachusetts prints *The Bay Psalm Book*, the first English-language book published in what is now the U.S.

1643 — Swedish settlers begin colonizing Pennsylvania.

About 1650 — North Carolina is colonized by Virginia settlers.

1660 — New Jersey colonization is begun by the Dutch at present-day Jersey City.

1670 — South Carolina colonization is begun by the English near Charleston.

1673 — Jacques Marquette and Louis Jolliet explore the upper Mississippi River for France.

1682—Philadelphia, Pennsylvania, is settled. La Salle explores Mississippi River all the way to its mouth in Louisiana and claims the whole Mississippi Valley for France.

1693—College of William and Mary is founded in Williamsburg, Virginia.

1700—Colonial population is about 250,000.

1703—Benjamin Franklin is born in Boston.

1732—George Washington, first president of the U.S., is born in Westmoreland County, Virginia.

1733—James Oglethorpe founds Savannah, Georgia; Georgia is established as the thirteenth colony.

1735—John Adams, second president of the U.S., is born in Braintree, Massachusetts.

1737—William Byrd founds Richmond, Virginia.

1738—British troops are sent to Georgia over border dispute with Spain.

1739—Black insurrection takes place in South Carolina.

1740—English Parliament passes act allowing naturalization of immigrants to American colonies after seven-year residence.

1743—Thomas Jefferson is born in Albemarle County, Virginia. Benjamin Franklin retires at age thirty-seven to devote himself to scientific inquiries and public service.

1744—King George's War begins; France joins war effort against England.

1745—During King George's War, France raids settlements in Maine and New York.

1747—Classes begin at Princeton College in New Jersey.

1748—The Treaty of Aix-la-Chapelle concludes King George's War.

1749—Parliament legally recognizes slavery in colonies and the inauguration of the plantation system in the South. George Washington becomes the surveyor for Culpepper County in Virginia.

1750—Thomas Walker passes through and names Cumberland Gap on his way toward Kentucky region. Colonial population is about 1,200,000.

1751—James Madison, fourth president of the U.S., is born in Port Conway, Virginia. English Parliament passes Currency Act, banning New England colonies from issuing paper money. George Washington travels to Barbados.

1752—Pennsylvania Hospital, the first general hospital in the colonies, is founded in Philadelphia. Benjamin Franklin uses a kite in a thunderstorm to demonstrate that lightning is a form of electricity.

1753—George Washington delivers command that the French withdraw from the Ohio River Valley; French disregard the demand. Colonial population is about 1,328,000.

1754—French and Indian War begins (extends to Europe as the Seven Years' War). Washington surrenders at Fort Necessity.

1755—French and Indians ambush Braddock. Washington becomes commander of Virginia troops.

1756—England declares war on France.

1758—James Monroe, fifth president of the U.S., is born in Westmoreland County, Virginia.

1759—Cherokee Indian war begins in southern colonies; hostilities extend to 1761. George Washington marries Martha Dandridge Custis.

1760—George III becomes king of England. Colonial population is about 1,600,000.

1762—England declares war on Spain.

1763—Treaty of Paris concludes the French and Indian War and the Seven Years' War. England gains Canada and most other French lands east of the Mississippi River.

1764—British pass the Sugar Act to gain tax money from the colonists. The issue of taxation without representation is first introduced in Boston. John Adams marries Abigail Smith.

1765—Stamp Act goes into effect in the colonies. Business virtually stops as almost all colonists refuse to use the stamps.

1766—British repeal the Stamp Act.

1767—John Quincy Adams, sixth president of the U.S. and son of second president John Adams, is born in Braintree, Massachusetts. Andrew Jackson, seventh president of the U.S., is born in Waxhaw settlement, South Carolina.

1769—Daniel Boone sights the Kentucky Territory.

1770—In the Boston Massacre, British soldiers kill five colonists and injure six. Townshend Acts are repealed, thus eliminating all duties on imports to the colonies except tea.

1771—Benjamin Franklin begins his autobiography, a work that he will never complete. The North Carolina assembly passes the "Bloody Act," which makes rioters guilty of treason.

1772—Samuel Adams rouses colonists to consider British threats to self-government.

1773—English Parliament passes the Tea Act. Colonists dressed as Mohawk Indians board British tea ships and toss 342 casks of tea into the water in what becomes known as the Boston Tea Party. William Henry Harrison is born in Charles City County, Virginia.

1774—British close the port of Boston to punish the city for the Boston Tea Party. First Continental Congress convenes in Philadelphia.

1775—American Revolution begins with battles of Lexington and Concord, Massachusetts. Second Continental Congress opens in Philadelphia. George Washington becomes commander-in-chief of the Continental army.

1776—Declaration of Independence is adopted on July 4.

1777—Congress adopts the American flag with thirteen stars and thirteen stripes. John Adams is sent to France to negotiate peace treaty.

1778—France declares war against Great Britain and becomes U.S. ally.

1779—British surrender to Americans at Vincennes. Thomas Jefferson is elected governor of Virginia. James Madison is elected to the Continental Congress.

1780—Benedict Arnold, first American traitor, defects to the British.

1781—Articles of Confederation go into effect. Cornwallis surrenders to George Washington at Yorktown, ending the American Revolution.

1782—American commissioners, including John Adams, sign peace treaty with British in Paris. Thomas Jefferson's wife, Martha, dies. Martin Van Buren is born in Kinderhook, New York.

1784—Zachary Taylor is born near Barboursville, Virginia.

1785—Congress adopts the dollar as the unit of currency. John Adams is made minister to Great Britain. Thomas Jefferson is appointed minister to France.

1786—Shays's Rebellion begins in Massachusetts.

1787—Constitutional Convention assembles in Philadelphia, with George Washington presiding; U.S. Constitution is adopted. Delaware, New Jersey, and Pennsylvania become states.

1788—Virginia, South Carolina, New York, Connecticut, New Hampshire, Maryland, and Massachusetts become states. U.S. Constitution is ratified. New York City is declared U.S. capital.

1789—Presidential electors elect George Washington and John Adams as first president and vice-president. Thomas Jefferson is appointed secretary of state. North Carolina becomes a state. French Revolution begins.

1790—Supreme Court meets for the first time. Rhode Island becomes a state. First national census in the U.S. counts 3,929,214 persons. John Tyler is born in Charles City County, Virginia.

1791—Vermont enters the Union. U.S. Bill of Rights, the first ten amendments to the Constitution, goes into effect. District of Columbia is established. James Buchanan is born in Stony Batter, Pennsylvania.

1792—Thomas Paine publishes *The Rights of Man*. Kentucky becomes a state. Two political parties are formed in the U.S., Federalist and Republican. Washington is elected to a second term, with Adams as vice-president.

1793—War between France and Britain begins; U.S. declares neutrality. Eli Whitney invents the cotton gin; cotton production and slave labor increase in the South.

1794—Eleventh Amendment to the Constitution is passed, limiting federal courts' power. "Whiskey Rebellion" in Pennsylvania protests federal whiskey tax. James Madison marries Dolley Payne Todd.

1795—George Washington signs the Jay Treaty with Great Britain. Treaty of San Lorenzo, between U.S. and Spain, settles Florida boundary and gives U.S. right to navigate the Mississippi. James Polk is born near Pineville, North Carolina.

1796—Tennessee enters the Union. Washington gives his Farewell Address, refusing a third presidential term. John Adams is elected president and Thomas Jefferson vice-president.

1797—Adams recommends defense measures against possible war with France. Napoleon Bonaparte and his army march against Austrians in Italy. U.S. population is about 4,900,000.

1798—Washington is named commander-in-chief of the U.S. Army. Department of the Navy is created. Alien and Sedition Acts are passed. Napoleon's troops invade Egypt and Switzerland.

1799—George Washington dies at Mount Vernon, New York. James Monroe is elected governor of Virginia. French Revolution ends. Napoleon becomes ruler of France.

1800—Thomas Jefferson and Aaron Burr tie for president. U.S. capital is moved from Philadelphia to Washington, D.C. The White House is built as presidents' home. Spain returns Louisiana to France. Millard Fillmore is born in Locke, New York.

1801—After thirty-six ballots, House of Representatives elects Thomas Jefferson president, making Burr vice-president. James Madison is named secretary of state.

1802—Congress abolishes excise taxes. U.S. Military Academy is founded at West Point, New York.

1803—Ohio enters the Union. Louisiana Purchase treaty is signed with France, greatly expanding U.S. territory.

1804—Twelfth Amendment to the Constitution rules that president and vice-president be elected separately. Alexander Hamilton is killed by Vice-President Aaron Burr in a duel. Orleans Territory is established. Napoleon crowns himself emperor of France. Franklin Pierce is born in Hillsborough Lower Village, New Hampshire.

1805—Thomas Jefferson begins his second term as president. Lewis and Clark expedition reaches the Pacific Ocean.

1806—Coinage of silver dollars is stopped; resumes in 1836.

1807—Aaron Burr is acquitted in treason trial. Embargo Act closes U.S. ports to trade.

1808—James Madison is elected president. Congress outlaws importing slaves from Africa. Andrew Johnson is born in Raleigh, North Carolina.

1809—Abraham Lincoln is born near Hodgenville, Kentucky.

1810—U.S. population is 7,240,000.

1811—William Henry Harrison defeats Indians at Tippecanoe. Monroe is named secretary of state.

1812—Louisiana becomes a state. U.S. declares war on Britain (War of 1812). James Madison is reelected president. Napoleon invades Russia.

1813—British forces take Fort Niagara and Buffalo, New York.

1814—Francis Scott Key writes "The Star-Spangled Banner." British troops burn much of Washington, D.C., including the White House. Treaty of Ghent ends War of 1812. James Monroe becomes secretary of war.

1815—Napoleon meets his final defeat at Battle of Waterloo.

1816—James Monroe is elected president. Indiana becomes a state.

1817—Mississippi becomes a state. Construction on Erie Canal begins.

1818—Illinois enters the Union. The present thirteen-stripe flag is adopted. Border between U.S. and Canada is agreed upon.

1819—Alabama becomes a state. U.S. purchases Florida from Spain. Thomas Jefferson establishes the University of Virginia.

1820—James Monroe is reelected. In the Missouri Compromise, Maine enters the Union as a free (non-slave) state.

1821—Missouri enters the Union as a slave state. Santa Fe Trail opens the American Southwest. Mexico declares independence from Spain. Napoleon Bonaparte dies.

1822—U.S. recognizes Mexico and Colombia. Liberia in Africa is founded as a home for freed slaves. Ulysses S. Grant is born in Point Pleasant, Ohio. Rutherford B. Hayes is born in Delaware, Ohio.

1823—Monroe Doctrine closes North and South America to European colonizing or invasion.

1824—House of Representatives elects John Quincy Adams president when none of the four candidates wins a majority in national election. Mexico becomes a republic.

1825—Erie Canal is opened. U.S. population is 11,300,000.

1826—Thomas Jefferson and John Adams both die on July 4, the fiftieth anniversary of the Declaration of Independence.

1828—Andrew Jackson is elected president. Tariff of Abominations is passed, cutting imports.

1829—James Madison attends Virginia's constitutional convention. Slavery is abolished in Mexico. Chester A. Arthur is born in Fairfield, Vermont.

1830—Indian Removal Act to resettle Indians west of the Mississippi is approved.

1831—James Monroe dies in New York City. James A. Garfield is born in Orange, Ohio. Cyrus McCormick develops his reaper.

1832—Andrew Jackson, nominated by the new Democratic Party, is reelected president.

1833—Britain abolishes slavery in its colonies. Benjamin Harrison is born in North Bend, Ohio.

1835—Federal government becomes debt-free for the first time.

1836—Martin Van Buren becomes president. Texas wins independence from Mexico. Arkansas joins the Union. James Madison dies at Montpelier, Virginia.

1837—Michigan enters the Union. U.S. population is 15,900,000. Grover Cleveland is born in Caldwell, New Jersey.

1840—William Henry Harrison is elected president.

1841—President Harrison dies in Washington, D.C., one month after inauguration. Vice-President John Tyler succeeds him.

1843—William McKinley is born in Niles, Ohio.

1844—James Knox Polk is elected president. Samuel Morse sends first telegraphic message.

1845—Texas and Florida become states. Potato famine in Ireland causes massive emigration from Ireland to U.S. Andrew Jackson dies near Nashville, Tennessee.

1846—Iowa enters the Union. War with Mexico begins.

1847—U.S. captures Mexico City.

1848—John Quincy Adams dies in Washington, D.C. Zachary Taylor becomes president. Treaty of Guadalupe Hidalgo ends Mexico-U.S. war. Wisconsin becomes a state.

1849—James Polk dies in Nashville, Tennessee.

1850—President Taylor dies in Washington, D.C.; Vice-President Millard Fillmore succeeds him. California enters the Union, breaking tie between slave and free states.

1852—Franklin Pierce is elected president.

1853—Gadsden Purchase transfers Mexican territory to U.S.

1854—"War for Bleeding Kansas" is fought between slave and free states.

1855—Czar Nicholas I of Russia dies, succeeded by Alexander II.

1856—James Buchanan is elected president. In Massacre of Potawatomi Creek, Kansas-slavers are murdered by free-staters. Woodrow Wilson is born in Staunton, Virginia.

1857—William Howard Taft is born in Cincinnati, Ohio.

1858—Minnesota enters the Union. Theodore Roosevelt is born in New York City.

1859—Oregon becomes a state.

1860—Abraham Lincoln is elected president; South Carolina secedes from the Union in protest.

1861—Arkansas, Tennessee, North Carolina, and Virginia secede. Kansas enters the Union as a free state. Civil War begins.

1862—Union forces capture Fort Henry, Roanoke Island, Fort Donelson, Jacksonville, and New Orleans; Union armies are defeated at the battles of Bull Run and Fredericksburg. Martin Van Buren dies in Kinderhook, New York. John Tyler dies near Charles City, Virginia.

1863—Lincoln issues Emancipation Proclamation: all slaves held in rebelling territories are declared free. West Virginia becomes a state.

1864—Abraham Lincoln is reelected. Nevada becomes a state.

1865—Lincoln is assassinated in Washington, D.C., and succeeded by Andrew Johnson. U.S. Civil War ends on May 26. Thirteenth Amendment abolishes slavery. Warren G. Harding is born in Blooming Grove, Ohio.

1867—Nebraska becomes a state. U.S. buys Alaska from Russia for $7,200,000. Reconstruction Acts are passed.

1868—President Johnson is impeached for violating Tenure of Office Act, but is acquitted by Senate. Ulysses S. Grant is elected president. Fourteenth Amendment prohibits voting discrimination. James Buchanan dies in Lancaster, Pennsylvania.

1869—Franklin Pierce dies in Concord, New Hampshire.

1870—Fifteenth Amendment gives blacks the right to vote.

1872—Grant is reelected over Horace Greeley. General Amnesty Act pardons ex-Confederates. Calvin Coolidge is born in Plymouth Notch, Vermont.

1874—Millard Fillmore dies in Buffalo, New York. Herbert Hoover is born in West Branch, Iowa.

1875—Andrew Johnson dies in Carter's Station, Tennessee.

1876—Colorado enters the Union. "Custer's last stand": he and his men are massacred by Sioux Indians at Little Big Horn, Montana.

1877—Rutherford B. Hayes is elected president as all disputed votes are awarded to him.

1880—James A. Garfield is elected president.

1881—President Garfield is assassinated and dies in Elberon, New Jersey. Vice-President Chester A. Arthur succeeds him.

1882—U.S. bans Chinese immigration. Franklin D. Roosevelt is born in Hyde Park, New York.

1884—Grover Cleveland is elected president. Harry S. Truman is born in Lamar, Missouri.

1885—Ulysses S. Grant dies in Mount McGregor, New York.

1886—Statue of Liberty is dedicated. Chester A. Arthur dies in New York City.

1888—Benjamin Harrison is elected president.

1889—North Dakota, South Dakota, Washington, and Montana become states.

1890—Dwight D. Eisenhower is born in Denison, Texas. Idaho and Wyoming become states.

1892—Grover Cleveland is elected president.

1893—Rutherford B. Hayes dies in Fremont, Ohio.

1896—William McKinley is elected president. Utah becomes a state.

1898—U.S. declares war on Spain over Cuba.

1900—McKinley is reelected. Boxer Rebellion against foreigners in China begins.

1901—McKinley is assassinated by anarchist Leon Czolgosz in Buffalo, New York; Theodore Roosevelt becomes president. Benjamin Harrison dies in Indianapolis, Indiana.

1902—U.S. acquires perpetual control over Panama Canal.

1903—Alaskan frontier is settled.

1904—Russian-Japanese War breaks out. Theodore Roosevelt wins presidential election.

1905—Treaty of Portsmouth signed, ending Russian-Japanese War.

1906—U.S. troops occupy Cuba.

1907—President Roosevelt bars all Japanese immigration. Oklahoma enters the Union.

1908—William Howard Taft becomes president. Grover Cleveland dies in Princeton, New Jersey. Lyndon B. Johnson is born near Stonewall, Texas.

1909—NAACP is founded under W.E.B. DuBois

1910—China abolishes slavery.

1911—Chinese Revolution begins. Ronald Reagan is born in Tampico, Illinois.

1912—Woodrow Wilson is elected president. Arizona and New Mexico become states.

1913—Federal income tax is introduced in U.S. through the Sixteenth Amendment. Richard Nixon is born in Yorba Linda, California. Gerald Ford is born in Omaha, Nebraska.

1914—World War I begins.

1915—British liner *Lusitania* is sunk by German submarine.

1916—Wilson is reelected president.

1917—U.S. breaks diplomatic relations with Germany. Czar Nicholas of Russia abdicates as revolution begins. U.S. declares war on Austria-Hungary. John F. Kennedy is born in Brookline, Massachusetts.

1918—Wilson proclaims "Fourteen Points" as war aims. On November 11, armistice is signed between Allies and Germany.

1919—Eighteenth Amendment prohibits sale and manufacture of intoxicating liquors. Wilson presides over first League of Nations; wins Nobel Peace Prize. Theodore Roosevelt dies in Oyster Bay, New York.

1920—Nineteenth Amendment (women's suffrage) is passed. Warren Harding is elected president.

1921—Adolf Hitler's stormtroopers begin to terrorize political opponents.

1922—Irish Free State is established. Soviet states form USSR. Benito Mussolini forms Fascist government in Italy.

1923—President Harding dies in San Francisco, California; he is succeeded by Vice-President Calvin Coolidge.

1924—Coolidge is elected president. Woodrow Wilson dies in Washington, D.C. James Carter is born in Plains, Georgia. George Bush is born in Milton, Massachusetts.

1925—Hitler reorganizes Nazi Party and publishes first volume of *Mein Kampf.*

1926—Fascist youth organizations founded in Germany and Italy. Republic of Lebanon proclaimed.

1927—Stalin becomes Soviet dictator. Economic conference in Geneva attended by fifty-two nations.

1928—Herbert Hoover is elected president. U.S. and many other nations sign Kellogg-Briand pacts to outlaw war.

1929—Stock prices in New York crash on "Black Thursday"; the Great Depression begins.

1930—Bank of U.S. and its many branches close (most significant bank failure of the year). William Howard Taft dies in Washington, D.C.

1931—Emigration from U.S. exceeds immigration for first time as Depression deepens.

1932—Franklin D. Roosevelt wins presidential election in a Democratic landslide.

1933—First concentration camps are erected in Germany. U.S. recognizes USSR and resumes trade. Twenty-First Amendment repeals prohibition. Calvin Coolidge dies in Northampton, Massachusetts.

1934—Severe dust storms hit Plains states. President Roosevelt passes U.S. Social Security Act.

1936—Roosevelt is reelected. Spanish Civil War begins. Hitler and Mussolini form Rome-Berlin Axis.

1937—Roosevelt signs Neutrality Act.

1938—Roosevelt sends appeal to Hitler and Mussolini to settle European problems amicably.

1939—Germany takes over Czechoslovakia and invades Poland, starting World War II.

1940—Roosevelt is reelected for a third term.

1941—Japan bombs Pearl Harbor; U.S. declares war on Japan. Germany and Italy declare war on U.S.; U.S. then declares war on them.

1942—Allies agree not to make separate peace treaties with the enemies. U.S. government transfers more than 100,000 Nisei (Japanese-Americans) from west coast to inland concentration camps.

1943—Allied bombings of Germany begin.

1944—Roosevelt is reelected for a fourth term. Allied forces invade Normandy on D-Day.

1945—President Franklin D. Roosevelt dies in Warm Springs, Georgia; Vice-President Harry S. Truman succeeds him. Mussolini is killed; Hitler commits suicide. Germany surrenders. U.S. drops atomic bomb on Hiroshima; Japan surrenders: end of World War II.

1946—U.N. General Assembly holds its first session in London. Peace conference of twenty-one nations is held in Paris.

1947—Peace treaties are signed in Paris. "Cold War" is in full swing.

1948—U.S. passes Marshall Plan Act, providing $17 billion in aid for Europe. U.S. recognizes new nation of Israel. India and Pakistan become free of British rule. Truman is elected president.

1949—Republic of Eire is proclaimed in Dublin. Russia blocks land route access from Western Germany to Berlin; airlift begins. U.S., France, and Britain agree to merge their zones of occupation in West Germany. Apartheid program begins in South Africa.

1950—Riots in Johannesburg, South Africa, against apartheid. North Korea invades South Korea. U.N. forces land in South Korea and recapture Seoul.

1951—Twenty-Second Amendment limits president to two terms.

1952—Dwight D. Eisenhower resigns as supreme commander in Europe and is elected president.

1953—Stalin dies; struggle for power in Russia follows. Rosenbergs are executed for espionage.

1954—U.S. and Japan sign mutual defense agreement.

1955—Blacks in Montgomery, Alabama, boycott segregated bus lines.

1956—Eisenhower is reelected president. Soviet troops march into Hungary.

1957—U.S. agrees to withdraw ground forces from Japan. Russia launches first satellite, *Sputnik.*

1958—European Common Market comes into being. Fidel Castro begins war against Batista government in Cuba.

1959—Alaska becomes the forty-ninth state. Hawaii becomes fiftieth state. Castro becomes premier of Cuba. De Gaulle is proclaimed president of the Fifth Republic of France.

1960—Historic debates between Senator John F. Kennedy and Vice-President Richard Nixon are televised. Kennedy is elected president. Brezhnev becomes president of USSR.

1961—Berlin Wall is constructed. Kennedy and Khrushchev confer in Vienna. In Bay of Pigs incident, Cubans trained by CIA attempt to overthrow Castro.

1962—U.S. military council is established in South Vietnam.

1963—Riots and beatings by police and whites mark civil rights demonstrations in Birmingham, Alabama; 30,000 troops are called out, Martin Luther King, Jr., is arrested. Freedom marchers descend on Washington, D.C., to demonstrate. President Kennedy is assassinated in Dallas, Texas; Vice-President Lyndon B. Johnson is sworn in as president.

1964—U.S. aircraft bomb North Vietnam. Johnson is elected president. Herbert Hoover dies in New York City.

1965—U.S. combat troops arrive in South Vietnam.

1966—Thousands protest U.S. policy in Vietnam. National Guard quells race riots in Chicago.

1967—Six-Day War between Israel and Arab nations.

1968—Martin Luther King, Jr., is assassinated in Memphis, Tennessee. Senator Robert Kennedy is assassinated in Los Angeles. Riots and police brutality take place at Democratic National Convention in Chicago. Richard Nixon is elected president. Czechoslovakia is invaded by Soviet troops.

1969—Dwight D. Eisenhower dies in Washington, D.C. Hundreds of thousands of people in several U.S. cities demonstrate against Vietnam War.

1970—Four Vietnam War protesters are killed by National Guardsmen at Kent State University in Ohio.

1971—Twenty-Sixth Amendment allows eighteen-year-olds to vote.

1972—Nixon visits Communist China; is reelected president in near-record landslide. Watergate affair begins when five men are arrested in the Watergate hotel complex in Washington, D.C. Nixon announces resignations of aides Haldeman, Ehrlichman, and Dean and Attorney General Kleindienst as a result of Watergate-related charges. Harry S. Truman dies in Kansas City, Missouri.

1973—Vice-President Spiro Agnew resigns; Gerald Ford is named vice-president. Vietnam peace treaty is formally approved after nineteen months of negotiations. Lyndon B. Johnson dies in San Antonio, Texas.

1974—As a result of Watergate cover-up, impeachment is considered; Nixon resigns and Ford becomes president. Ford pardons Nixon and grants limited amnesty to Vietnam War draft evaders and military deserters.

1975—U.S. civilians are evacuated from Saigon, South Vietnam, as Communist forces complete takeover of South Vietnam.

1976—U.S. celebrates its Bicentennial. James Earl Carter becomes president.

1977—Carter pardons most Vietnam draft evaders, numbering some 10,000.

1980—Ronald Reagan is elected president.

1981—President Reagan is shot in the chest in assassination attempt. Sandra Day O'Connor is appointed first woman justice of the Supreme Court.

1983—U.S. troops invade island of Grenada.

1984—Reagan is reelected president. Democratic candidate Walter Mondale's running mate, Geraldine Ferraro, is the first woman selected for vice-president by a major U.S. political party.

1985—Soviet Communist Party secretary Konstantin Chernenko dies; Mikhail Gorbachev succeeds him. U.S. and Soviet officials discuss arms control in Geneva. Reagan and Gorbachev hold summit conference in Geneva. Racial tensions accelerate in South Africa.

1986—Space shuttle *Challenger* explodes shortly after takeoff; crew of seven dies. U.S. bombs bases in Libya. Corazon Aquino defeats Ferdinand Marcos in Philippine presidential election.

1987—Iraqi missile rips the U.S. frigate *Stark* in the Persian Gulf, killing thirty-seven American sailors. Congress holds hearings to investigate sale of U.S. arms to Iran to finance Nicaraguan *contra* movement.

1988—George Bush is elected president. President Reagan and Soviet leader Gorbachev sign INF treaty, eliminating intermediate nuclear forces. Severe drought sweeps the United States.

1989—East Germany opens Berlin Wall, allowing citizens free exit. Communists lose control of governments in Poland, Romania, and Czechoslovakia. Chinese troops massacre over 1,000 pro-democracy student demonstrators in Beijing's Tiananmen Square.

1990—Iraq annexes Kuwait, provoking the threat of war. East and West Germany are reunited. The Cold War between the United States and the Soviet Union comes to a close. Several Soviet republics make moves toward independence.

1991—Backed by a coalition of members of the United Nations, U.S. troops drive Iraquis from Kuwait. Latvia, Lithuania, and Estonia withdraw from the U.S.S.R. The Soviet Union dissolves as its republics secede to form a commonwealth of free nations.

1992—U.N. forces fail to stop fighting in territories of former Yugoslavia. More than fifty people are killed and more than six hundred buildings burned in rioting in Los Angeles. U.S. unemployment reaches eight-year high. Hurricane Andrew devastates southern Florida and parts of Louisiana. International relief supplies and troops are sent to combat famine and violence in Somalia.

1993—U.S.-led forces use airplanes and missiles to attack military targets in Iraq. William Jefferson Clinton becomes the forty-second U.S. president.

Index

Page numbers in boldface type indicate illustrations.

About the Author

Linda R. Wade is a school librarian and free-lance writer living in Fort Wayne, Indiana. Her work has appeared in a number of journals and other publications. As an instructor and lecturer, she has contributed to many writers' conferences and workshops. Ms. Wade's position as a media specialist in an elementary school library has enriched her interest in, and love for, children's literature.